Fun at the Beach

Johanna Rohan

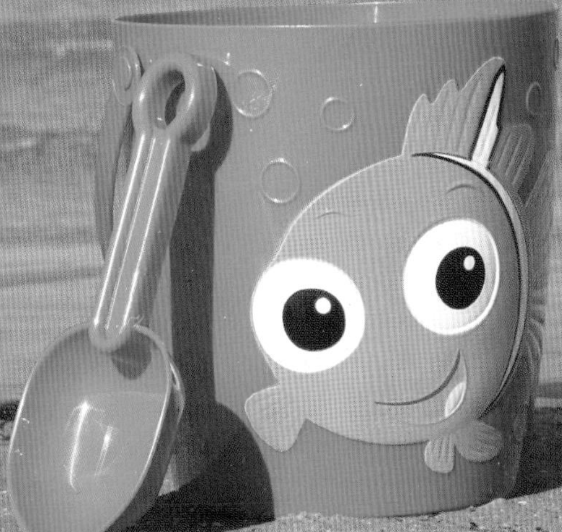

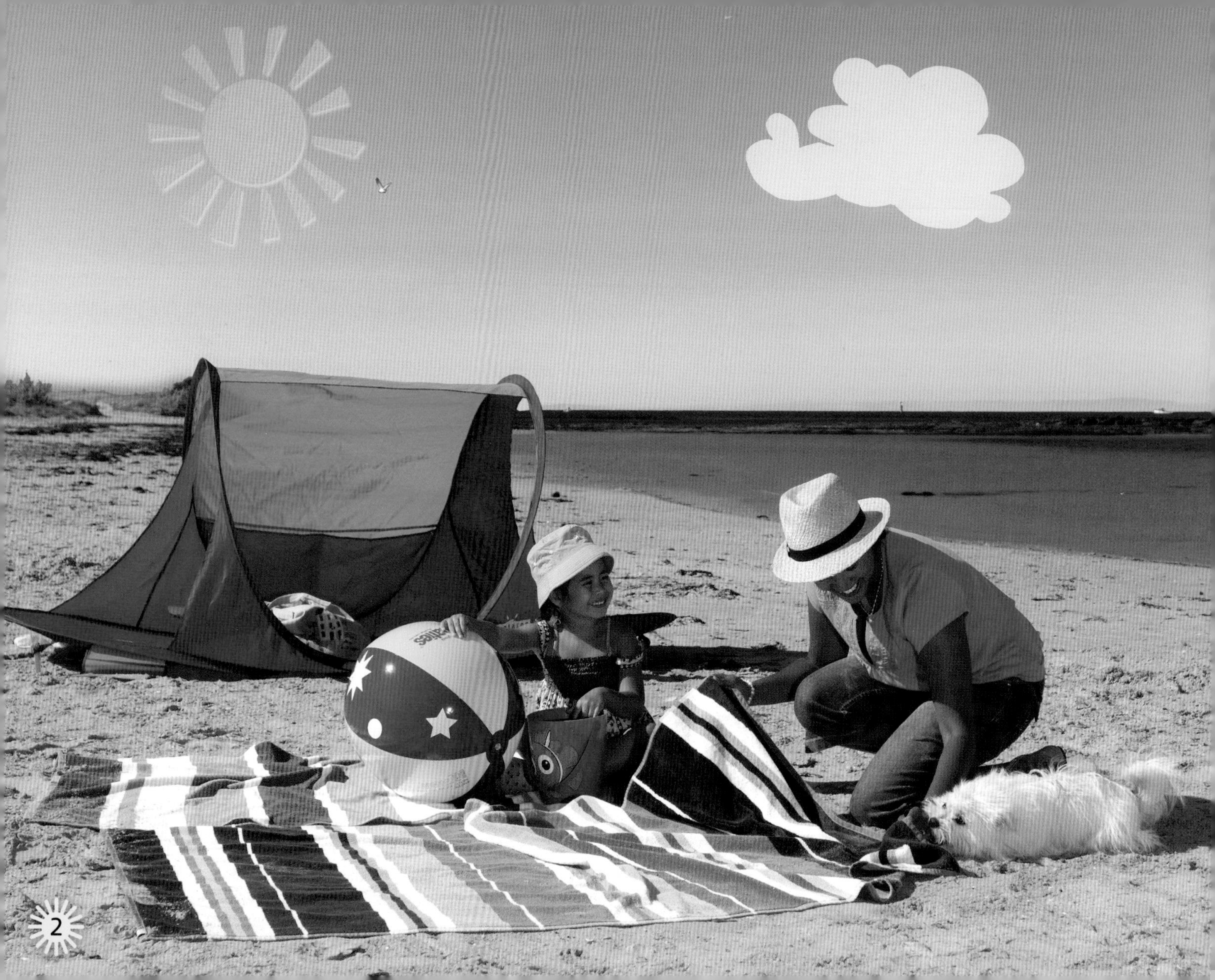

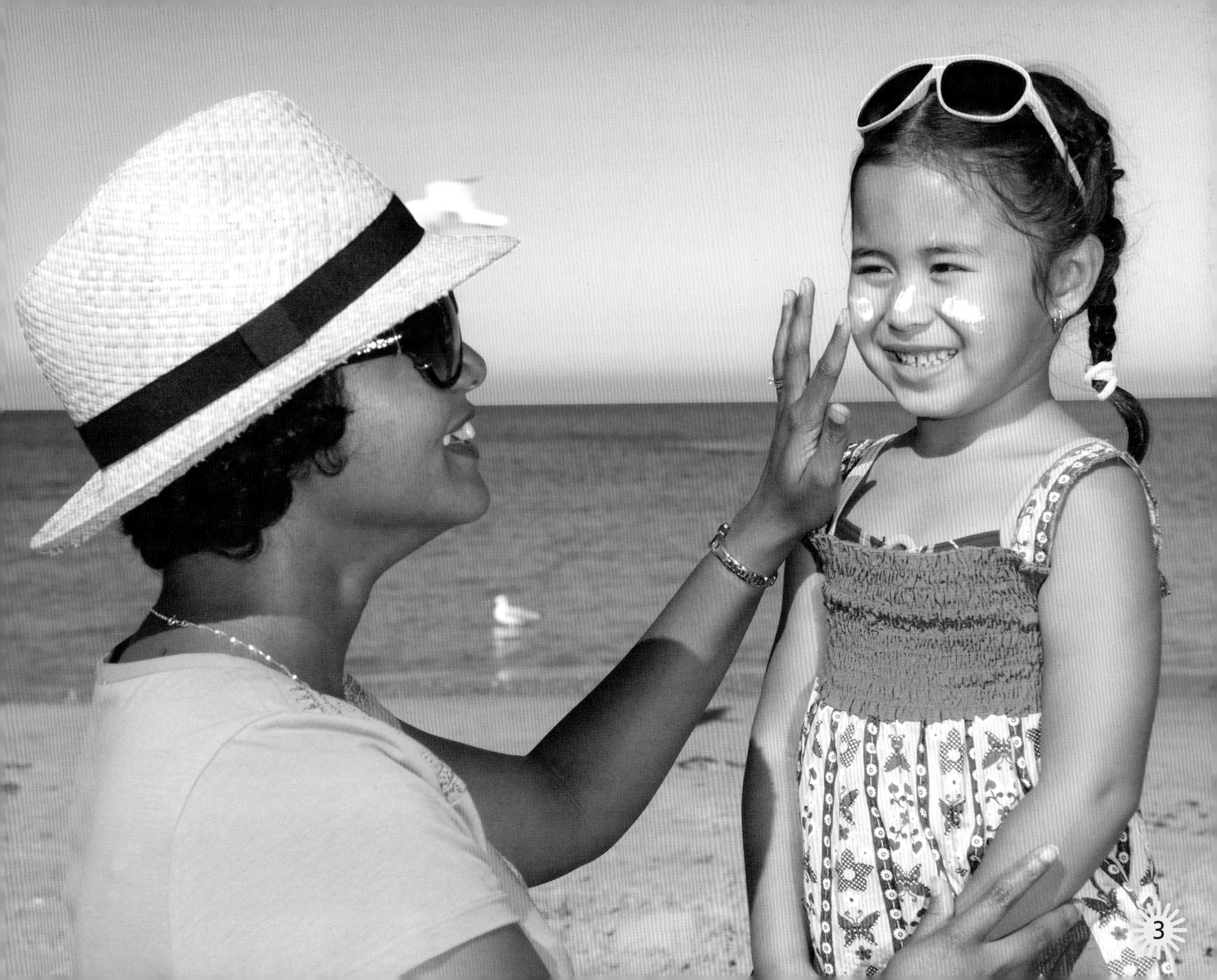

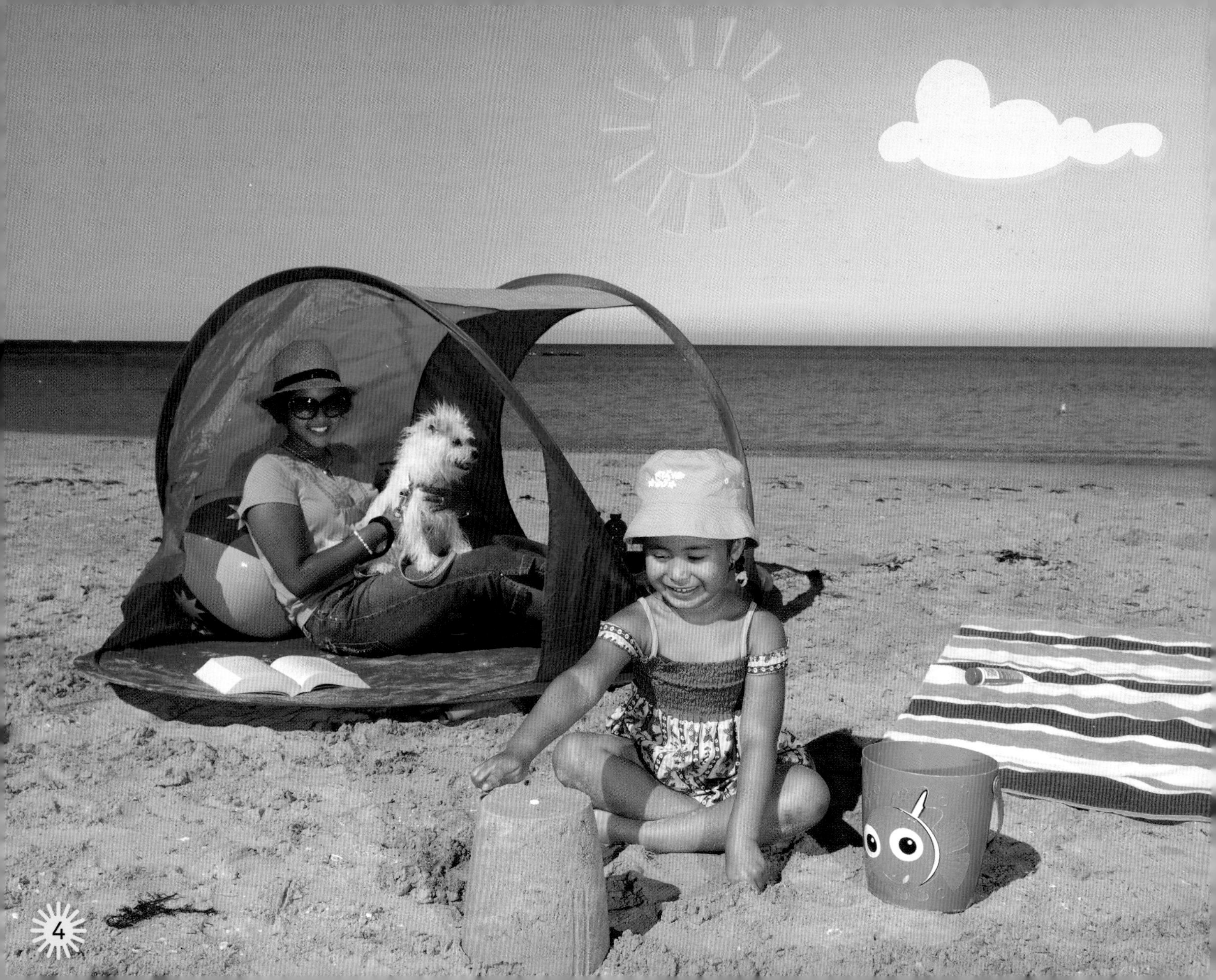

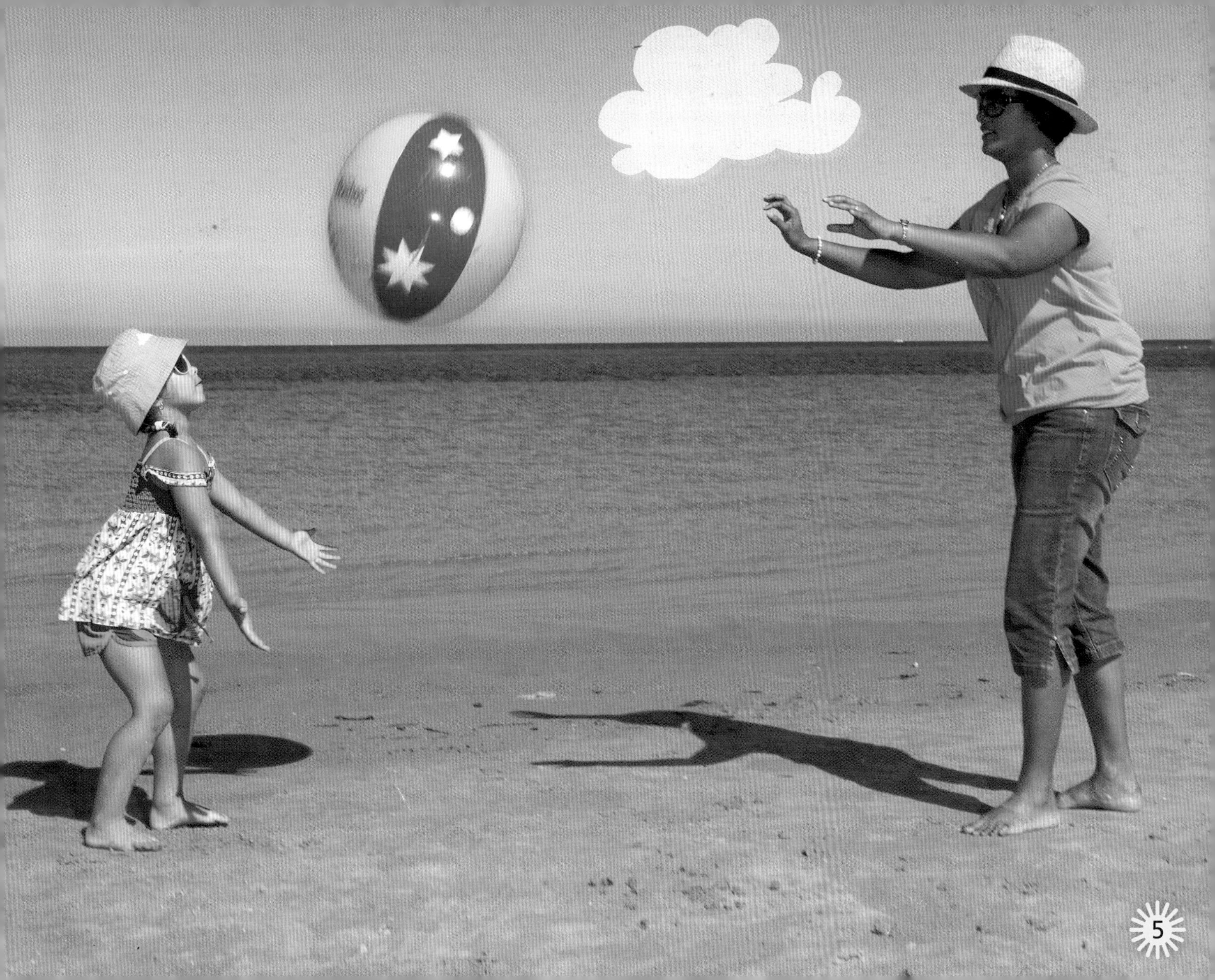

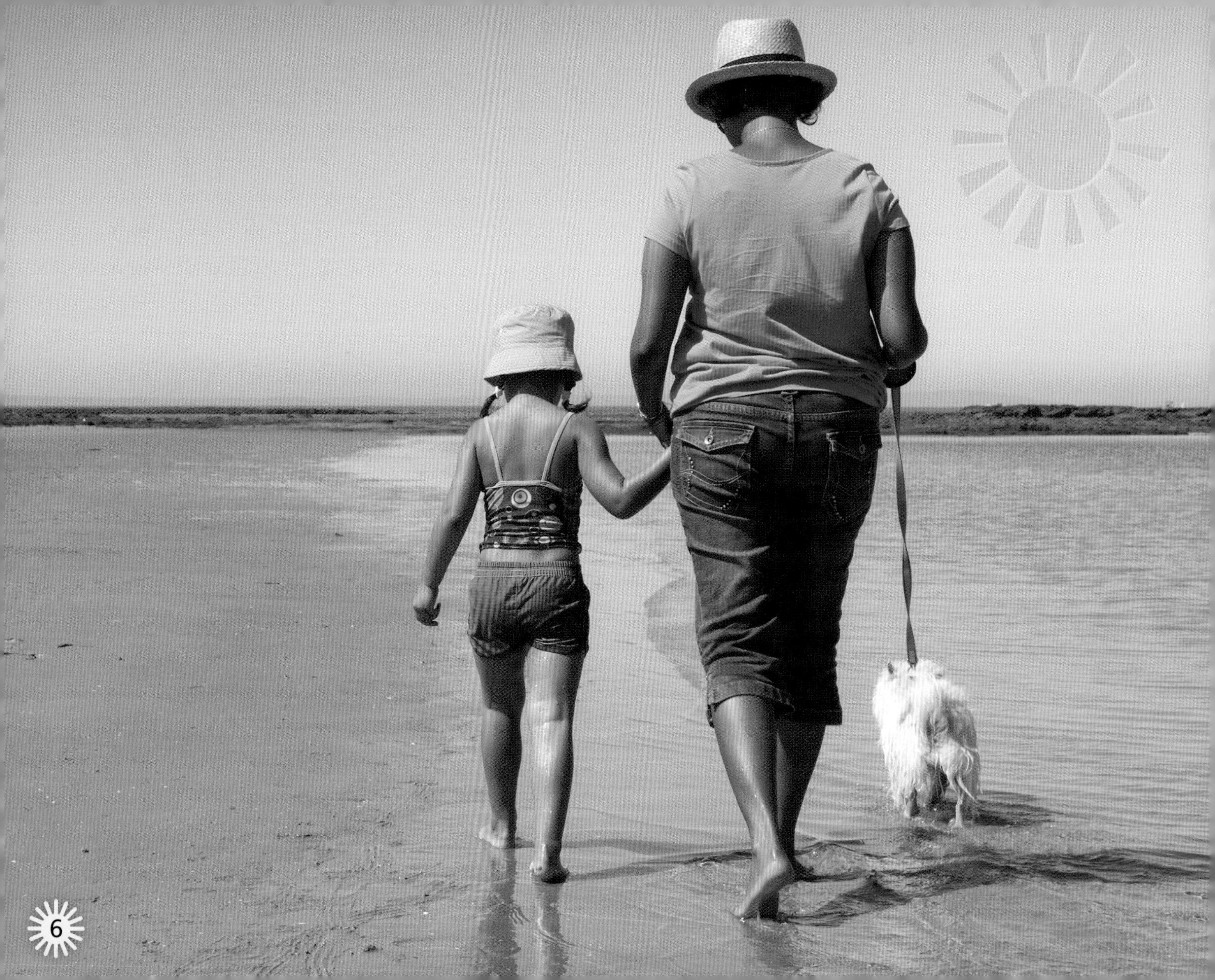

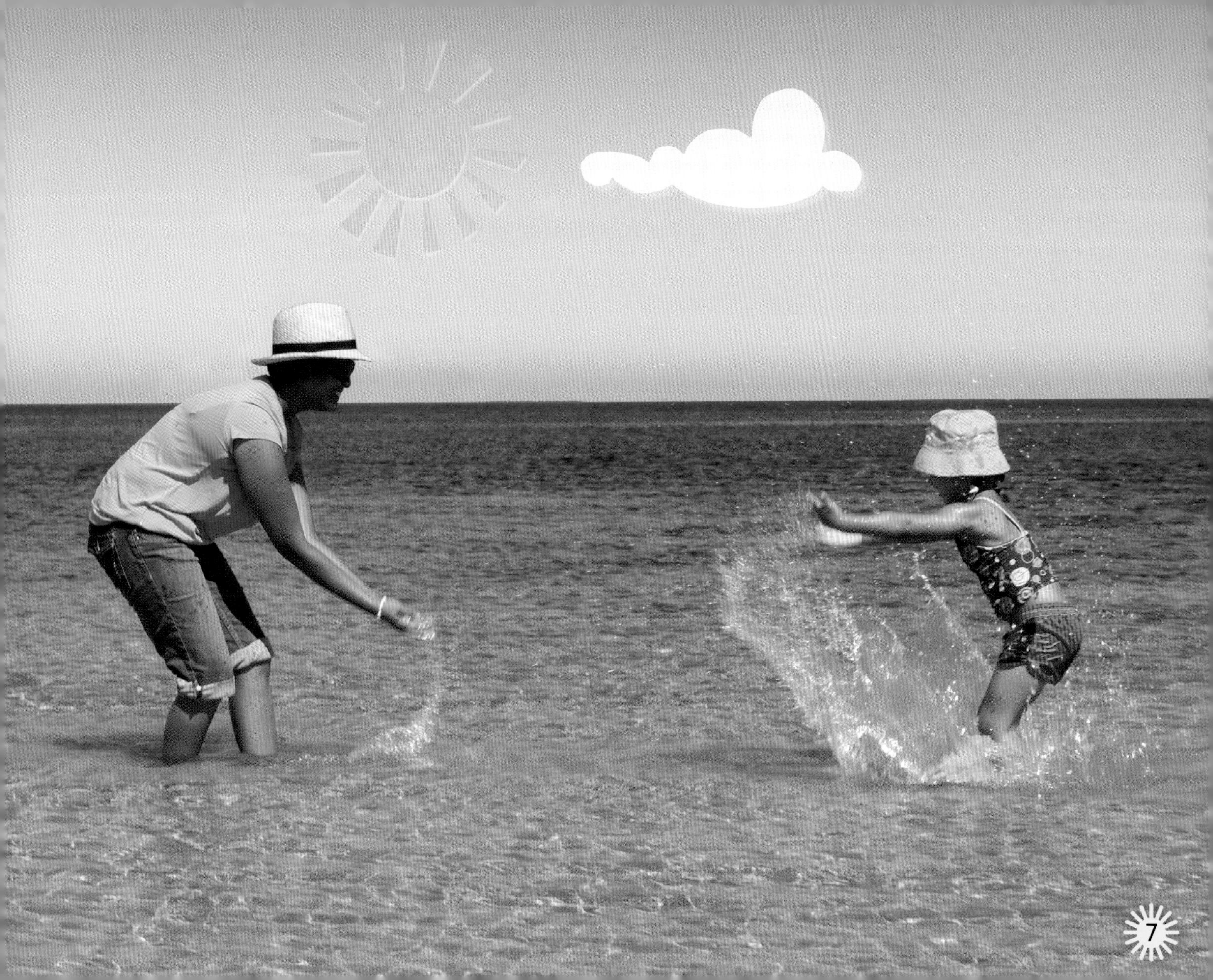

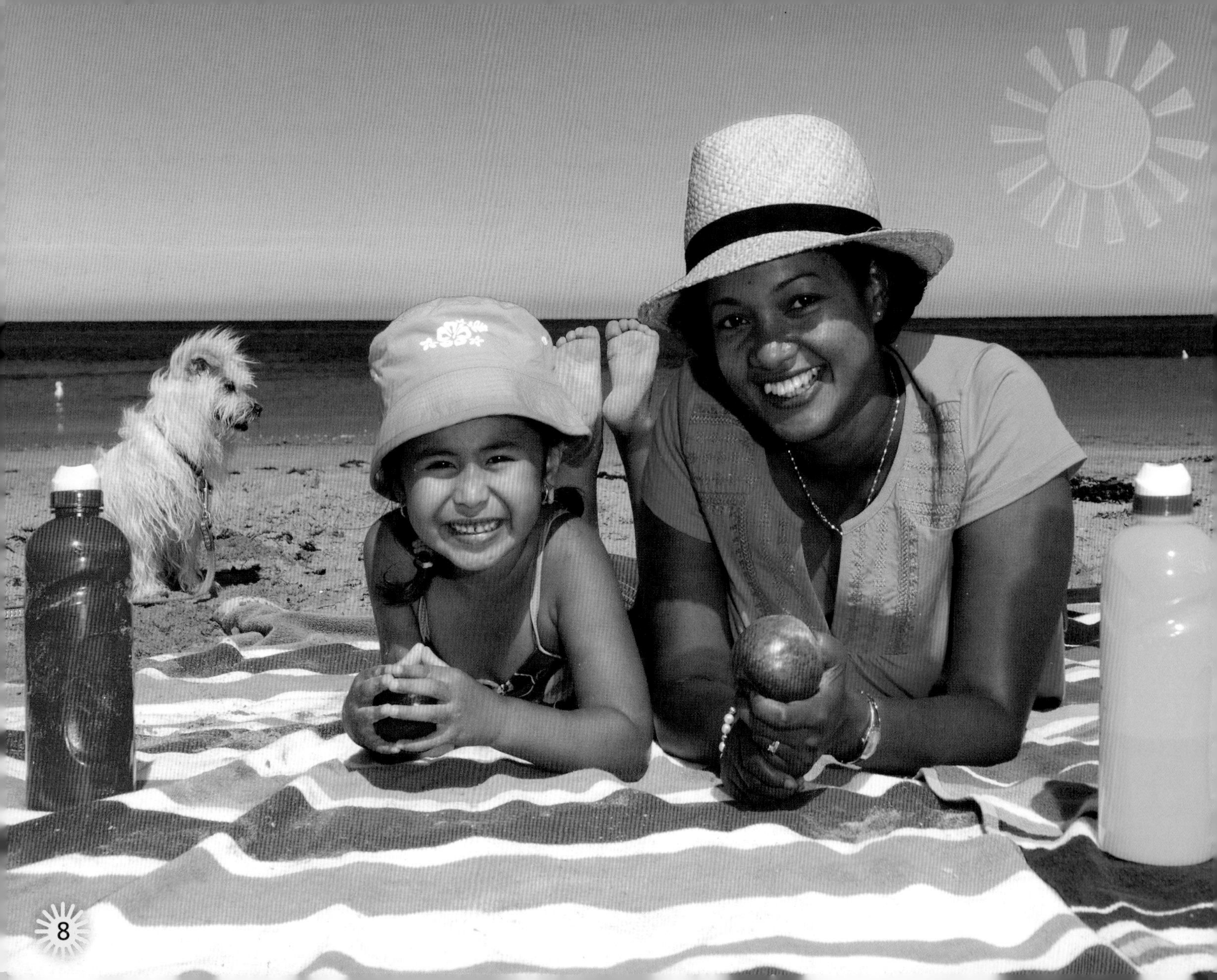